I Believe...

I am a Seventh Day Adventist

This journal belongs to:

by Beverly Dabney Becton, Ph.D.

I BELIEVE...I AM A SEVENTH DAY ADVENTIST
I Believe Series: SDA Journal

© Copyrights 2018 by Beverly Dabney Becton, Ph.D.

All rights reserved. No part of this publication may be reproduced, distributed, or transmitted in any form or by any means, including photocopying, recording, or other electronic or mechanical methods, without the prior written permission of the publisher or author.

Scriptures marked KJV are taken from the KING JAMES VERSION (KJV): KING JAMES VERSION, public domain.

Scriptures marked NIV are taken from the NEW INTERNATIONAL VERSION (NIV): Scripture taken from THE HOLY BIBLE, NEW INTERNATIONAL VERSION ®. Copyright© 1973, 1978, 1984, 2011 by Biblica, Inc.™ Used by permission of Zondervan.

Scripture taken from the NEW KING JAMES VERSION®. Copyright© 1982 by Thomas Nelson. Used by permission. All rights reserved.

Published by:
Watersprings Media House, LLC
P.O. Box 1284
Olive Branch, MS 38654
For permission requests and bulk orders contact publisher.
www.waterspringsmedia.com

ISBN 13: 978-1-948877-00-8

Printed in the United States of America.

Introduction
The Seventh Day Adventist Church

Founders of the Adventist Church were formerly part of the Millerite movement in the 1840's, who believed Jesus Christ would return in October 1844. In 1844, after the great disappointment, the Millerite movement splintered; however, a small group, who became the nucleus of the Adventist Church, continued studying the Bible and its prophetic message of the second coming of Jesus. Among the pioneers and future leaders of the church were Ellen Harmon (White), James White, Joseph Bates, Uriah Smith, John Nevins Andrews, George Butler and others. They rallied behind biblical truths achieved through prayer, bible study, or revealed through prophecy. The publishing ministry became the vehicle to share these truths and coalesce members throughout the United States.

The Seventh Day Adventist Church (SDA) adopted its name in 1860 and in 1863 organized as a church from groups of seventh-day Sabbatarian Adventist believers located across the United States. The General Conference of SDA was formed in 1863 with a mission focus of sharing the good news of Jesus Christ, declaring salvation for all.

In 1874, the Adventist Church began its world-wide church by launching its first overseas mission. During the year of 1903, the Adventist Church had reached 70 of the world's countries. By 2015, the church's outreach to all people had resulted in churches and companies in 215 out of the 237 countries and areas of the world recognized by the United Nations.

William A. Spicer, former church president and former missionary to India, stated in a 1921 speech, *"Mission is not something in addition to the regular work of the church. The work of God is one work, the wide world over… To carry the one message of salvation to all peoples … is the aim of every conference, every church, and every believer."* The SDA Church continues the mission of spreading the "Good News" of salvation *for all* through Jesus Christ our Lord.

The pages of this journal contain the beliefs of the Seventh Day Adventist Church. Seventh-day Adventists accept the Bible as the only source of their beliefs. The SDA church has agreed upon key statements that summarize the principal teachings the church understands from the Bible. These principal teachings are presented as 28 fundamental beliefs.

https://www.adventist.org/en/beliefs/

https://www.adventist.org/en/information/history/

https://www.adventist.org/en/information/statistics/article/go/-/seventh-day-adventist-world-church-statistics-2015/

http://www.whiteestate.org

What Seventh Day Adventist Believe: 28 FUNDAMENTAL BELIEFS

1. The Holy Scriptures
2. The Trinity
3. The Father
4. The Son
5. The Holy Spirit
6. Creation
7. The Nature of Humanity
8. The Great Controversy
9. The Life, Death, and Resurrection of Christ
10. The Experience of Salvation
11. The Growing in Christ
12. The Church
13. The Remnant and Its Mission
14. Unity in the Body of Christ
15. Baptism
16. The Lord's Supper
17. Spiritual Gifts and Ministries
18. The Gift of Prophecy
19. The Law of God
20. The Sabbath
21. Stewardship
22. Christian Behavior
23. Marriage and the Family
24. Christ's Ministry in the Heavenly Sanctuary
25. The Second Coming of Christ
26. Death and Resurrection
27. The Millennium and the End of Sin
28. The New Earth

www.adventist.org

Introduction to the Journal

A very good friend of mine shared with me that we should support God's word by giving three witnesses (texts) from the bible. Throughout the Bible, there are various examples of the power of two or three witnesses (2 Corinthians 13:1; Matthew 18: 15, 16; 1 John 5:7 and Hebrews 10:28).

In this journal each of the 28 fundamental beliefs will be supported by three scriptures; one taken from each of the following Bible translations: the King James Version, the New International Version, and the New King James Version. There are a total of 84 scriptures here-in. (Additional scriptures on each belief are located in the Study Resource pages found in the back of the journal.)

How to Use This Journal

- Personal Journal/Diary - Record your ideas, experiences, hopes and dreams
- Study Journal – Study the Doctrines
    a. How do they impact my life?
    b. How can I become a better witness for Christ?
    c. How can I better understand the beliefs of the SDA Church?
- Writing Tool – Record content of your choosing
    a. sermon notes
    b. work information
    c. family history
- Artist Journal - Record drawings, illustrations, post pictures, use for other visual systems
- Witnessing Tool - Share God's Word by gifting it to others

Study to show thyself approved unto God, a workman that needeth not to be ashamed, rightly dividing the word of truth.

2 Timothy 2:15 (KJV)

King James Version

> For the prophecy came not in old time by the will of man:
> But holy men of God spake as they were moved by the Holy Ghost.
> *2 Peter 1:21 (KJV)*

THE HOLY SCRIPTURES
I AM A SEVENTH-DAY ADVENTIST

> For there are three that bear record
> in Heaven, the Father, The Word, and the Holy Ghost:
> and these three are one.
> *1 John 5:7 (KJV)*

THE TRINITY
I AM A SEVENTH-DAY ADVENTIST

> O righteous Father, the world hath not known thee:
> but I have known thee, and these have
> known that thou hast sent me.
> *John 17:25 (KJV)*

3

THE FATHER
I AM A SEVENTH-DAY ADVENTIST

And the word was made flesh, and dwelt among us, (and we beheld his glory, the glory as of the only begotten of the Father,) full of grace and truth.
John 1:14 (KJV)

 **THE SON**
I AM A SEVENTH-DAY ADVENTIST

And when they had prayed, the place was shaken where they were assembled together; and they were all filled with the Holy Ghost, and they spake the word of God with boldness.
Acts 4:31 (KJV)

5

THE HOLY SPIRIT
I AM A SEVENTH-DAY ADVENTIST

> The LORD by wisdom hath founded the earth;
> by understanding hath he established the heavens.
> *Proverbs 3:19 (KJV)*

CREATION
I AM A SEVENTH-DAY ADVENTIST

> So God created man in his own image, in
> the image of God created he him;
> male and female created he them.
> *Genesis 1:27 (KJV)*

THE NATURE OF HUMANITY
I AM A SEVENTH-DAY ADVENTIST

> For we wrestle not against flesh and blood, but against principalities, against powers, against the rulers of the darkness of this world, against spiritual wickedness in high places.
> *Ephesians 6:12 (KJV)*

> He is not here, but is risen: remember how he spake
> unto you when he was yet in Galilee,
> saying, the Son of Man must be delivered into the
> hands of sinful men, and be crucified, and the third day rise again.
> *Luke 24:6-7 (KJV)*

THE LIFE, DEATH, AND RESURRECTION OF CHRIST
I AM A SEVENTH-DAY ADVENTIST

...And if any man sin, we have an advocate with the Father, Jesus Christ the righteous: And He is the propitiation for our sins: and not for ours only, but also for the sins of the whole world.
1 John 2:1b-2 (KJV)

> As obedient children, not fashioning yourselves according to the former lusts in your ignorance: but as he which hath called you is holy, so be ye holy in all manner of conversation
>
> *1 Peter 1:14 15 (KJV)*

> Peter therefore was kept in prison:
> but prayer was made without ceasing
> of the church unto God for him.
> *Acts 12:5 (KJV)*

THE CHURCH
I AM A SEVENTH-DAY ADVENTIST

> Then Philip opened his mouth, and
> began at the same scripture, and preached unto him Jesus.
> *Acts 8:35 (KJV)*

13

 **THE REMNANT AND ITS MISSION**
I AM A SEVENTH-DAY ADVENTIST

> With all lowliness and meekness,
> with longsuffering, forbearing one another
> in love; endeavoring to keep the
> unity of the Spirit in the bond of peace.
> *Ephesians 4:2-3 (KJV)*

> Then Peter said unto them, Repent, and be baptized every one of you in the name of Jesus Christ for the remission of sins, and ye shall receive the gift of the Holy Ghost.
> *Acts 2:38 (KJV)*

BAPTISM
I AM A SEVENTH-DAY ADVENTIST

> And he took bread, and gave thanks, and brake it, and gave unto them, saying, This is my body which is given for you: this do in remembrance of me.
> *Luke 22:19 (KJV)*

 **THE LORD'S SUPPER**
I AM A SEVENTH-DAY ADVENTIST

Wherefore He saith, When he ascended up on high,
he led captivity captive, and gave gifts unto men.
Ephesians 4:8 (KJV)

SPIRITUAL GIFTS AND MINISTRIES
I AM A SEVENTH-DAY ADVENTIST

> ...And we entered into the house of Philip the evangelist, which was one of the seven; and abode with him. And the same man had four daughters, virgins, which did prophesy.
> *Acts 21: 8b-9 (KJV)*

THE GIFT OF PROPHECY
I AM A SEVENTH-DAY ADVENTIST

> I delight to do thy will, O my God:
> yea, thy law is within my heart.
> *Psalms 40:8 (KJV)*

THE LAW OF GOD
I AM A SEVENTH-DAY ADVENTIST

> For he spake in a certain place of the seventh day on this wise, And God did rest the seventh day from all his works.
> *Hebrews 4:4 (KJV)*

THE SABBATH
I AM A SEVENTH-DAY ADVENTIST

> Honour The Lord with thy substance,
> and with the firstfruits of all thine increase.
> *Proverbs 3:9 (KJV)*

STEWARDSHIP
I AM A SEVENTH-DAY ADVENTIST

> Beloved, let us love one another: for love is of God; and every one that loveth is born of God, and knoweth God.
> *1 John 4:7 (KJV)*

CHRISTIAN BEHAVIOR
I AM A SEVENTH-DAY ADVENTIST

> Marriage is honourable in all,
> and the bed undefiled.
> *Hebrews 13:4a (KJV)*

MARRIAGE AND THE FAMILY
I AM A SEVENTH-DAY ADVENTIST

> For there is one God, and one mediator between God and men, the man Christ Jesus.
> *1 Timothy 2:5 (KJV)*

CHRIST'S MINISTRY IN THE HEAVENLY SANCTUARY
I AM A SEVENTH-DAY ADVENTIST

> Behold, he cometh with clouds;
> and every eye shall see him...
> *Revelation 1:7a (KJV)*

THE SECOND COMING OF CHRIST
I AM A SEVENTH-DAY ADVENTIST

> Why should it be thought a thing incredible with you, that God should raise the dead?
> *Acts 26:8 (KJV)*

> And He laid hold on the dragon, that old serpent, which is the Devil, and Satan, and bound him a thousand years.
> *Revelation 20:2 (KJV)*

THE MILLENNIUM AND THE END OF SIN
I AM A SEVENTH-DAY ADVENTIST

> For, behold, I create new heavens and a new earth: and the former shall not be remembered, nor come into mind.
> *Isaiah 65:17 (KJV)*

THE NEW EARTH
I AM A SEVENTH-DAY ADVENTIST

Do your best to present yourself to God as one approved, a worker who does not need to be ashamed and who correctly handles the word of truth.

2 Timothy 2:15 (NIV)

New International Version

> All scripture is God-breathed and is useful for teaching, rebuking, correcting and training in righteousness.
> *2 Timothy 3:16 (NIV)*

THE HOLY SCRIPTURES
I AM A SEVENTH-DAY ADVENTIST

> May the Grace of the Lord Jesus Christ, and the love of God, and the fellowship of the Holy Spirit be with you all.
> *2 Corinthians 13:14 (NIV)*

THE TRINITY
I AM A SEVENTH-DAY ADVENTIST

> This is how God showed his love among us:
> He sent his one and only Son into the world
> that we might live through him.
> *1 John 4:9 (NIV)*

THE FATHER
I AM A SEVENTH-DAY ADVENTIST

> And a voice from heaven said,
> "This is my Son, whom I love;
> with him I am well pleased."
> *Matthew 3:17 (NIV)*

4

 **THE SON**
I AM A SEVENTH-DAY ADVENTIST

> But you will receive power when
> the Holy Spirit comes on you...
> *Acts 1:8a (NIV)*

THE HOLY SPIRIT
I AM A SEVENTH-DAY ADVENTIST

> In the beginning God created the heavens and the earth.
> *Genesis 1:1 (NIV)*

CREATION
I AM A SEVENTH-DAY ADVENTIST

> I have been crucified with Christ
> and I no longer live, but Christ lives in me.
> The life I now live in the body, I live by faith
> in the Son of God, who loved me and
> gave himself for me.
> *Galatians 2:20 (NIV)*

THE NATURE OF HUMANITY
I AM A SEVENTH-DAY ADVENTIST

> Then war broke out in heaven. Michael and his angels fought against the dragon, and the dragon and his angels fought back.
> *Revelation 12:7 (NIV)*

> ...That Christ died for our sins according to the Scriptures, that he was buried, that he was raised on the third day according to the Scriptures...
> *1 Corinthians 15:3a-4 (NIV)*

THE LIFE, DEATH, AND RESURRECTION OF CHRIST
I AM A SEVENTH-DAY ADVENTIST

> For God so loved the world that
> he gave his one and only Son, that
> whoever believes in him shall not perish
> but have eternal life.
> *John 3:16 (NIV)*

> But grow in the grace and knowledge
> of our Lord and Savior Jesus Christ.
> *2 Peter 3:18 (NIV)*

THE GROWING IN CHRIST
I AM A SEVENTH-DAY ADVENTIST

> His intent was that now, through the church,
> the manifold wisdom of God should be
> made known to the Rulers and Authorities
> in the Heavenly Realms
>
> *Ephesians 3:10 (NIV)*

THE CHURCH
I AM A SEVENTH-DAY ADVENTIST

> Therefore go and make disciples of
> all nations, baptizing them in the name of
> the Father and of the Son and of the Holy Spirit, and
> teaching them to obey everything
> I have commanded you....
> *Matthew 28:19-20a (NIV)*

THE REMNANT AND ITS MISSION
I AM A SEVENTH-DAY ADVENTIST

> So in Christ we, though many, form One body, and each member belongs to all the others.
> *Romans 12:5 (NIV)*

UNITY IN THE BODY OF CHRIST
I AM A SEVENTH-DAY ADVENTIST

> Whoever believes and is baptized
> will be saved...
> *Mark 16:16a (NIV)*

___

BAPTISM
I AM A SEVENTH-DAY ADVENTIST

> For whenever you eat this bread
> and drink this cup, you proclaim the Lord's
> death until he comes.
> *1 Corinthians 11:26 (NIV)*

THE LORD'S SUPPER
I AM A SEVENTH-DAY ADVENTIST

> There are different kinds of gifts,
> But the same spirit distributes them.
> There are different kinds of service,
> But the same Lord.
> *1 Corinthians 12:4-5 (NIV)*

SPIRITUAL GIFTS AND MINISTRIES
I AM A SEVENTH-DAY ADVENTIST

> Follow the way of love and eagerly desire
> gifts of the Spirit, especially prophecy.
> But the one who prophesies speaks to people
> for their strengthening, encouraging and comfort.
> *1 Corinthians 14:1, 3 (NIV)*

THE GIFT OF PROPHECY
I AM A SEVENTH-DAY ADVENTIST

> Do not think that I have come to abolish
> the Law or the prophets; I have not come to abolish them
> but to fulfill them.
> *Matthew 5:17 (NIV)*

THE LAW OF GOD
I AM A SEVENTH-DAY ADVENTIST

> Remember the Sabbath day by keeping it holy.
> *Exodus 20:8 (NIV)*

THE SABBATH
I AM A SEVENTH-DAY ADVENTIST

"Bring the whole tithe into the storehouse, that there may be food in my house. Test me in this," says the Lord Almighty, "and see if I will not throw open the floodgates of heaven and pour out so much blessing that there will not be room enough to store it.
Malachi 3:10 (NIV)

STEWARDSHIP
I AM A SEVENTH-DAY ADVENTIST

> Do not conform to the
> pattern of this world, but be
> transformed by the renewing of your mind.
> *Romans 12:2 (NIV)*

CHRISTIAN BEHAVIOR
I AM A SEVENTH-DAY ADVENTIST

> Do not be yoked together with unbelievers.
> For what do righteousness and wickedness have in common?
> *2 Corinthians 6:14a (NIV)*

MARRIAGE AND THE FAMILY
I AM A SEVENTH-DAY ADVENTIST

> We do have such a high priest, who sat down at the right hand of the throne of the Majesty in heaven, and who serves in the sanctuary.
> *Hebrews 8:1b- 2a (NIV)*

> For the Lord himself will come down from heaven, with a loud command, With the voice of the archangel and with the trumpet call of God, and the dead in Christ will rise first.
> *1 Thessalonians 4:16 (NIV)*

THE SECOND COMING OF CHRIST
I AM A SEVENTH-DAY ADVENTIST

> Listen, I tell you a mystery: We will not all sleep,
> but we will all be changed – in a flash, in the twinkling of
> an eye, at the last trumpet. For the trumpet will sound,
> the dead will be raised imperishable, and we will be changed.
> *1 Corinthians 15:51-52 (NIV)*

DEATH AND RESURRECTION
I AM A SEVENTH-DAY ADVENTIST

> Blessed and holy are those who share in the first resurrection. The second death has no power over them, but they will be priests of God and of Christ and will reign with him for a thousand years.
> *Revelation 20:6 (NIV)*

> But in keeping with his promise we are looking forward to a new heaven and a new earth, where righteousness dwells.
> *2 Peter 3:13 (NIV)*

THE NEW EARTH
I AM A SEVENTH-DAY ADVENTIST

Be diligent to present yourself approved to God, a worker who does not need to be ashamed, rightly dividing the word of truth.

2 Timothy 2:15 (NKJV)

New King James Version

> You search the Scriptures, for in them you think you have eternal life; and these are they which testify of Me.
> *John 5:39 (NKJV)*

1

THE HOLY SCRIPTURES
I AM A SEVENTH-DAY ADVENTIST

> And the Holy Spirit descended in bodily form like a dove upon Him, and a voice came from Heaven which said, "You are my Beloved Son, in You I am well pleased."
> *Luke 3:22 (NKJV)*

2

THE TRINITY
I AM A SEVENTH-DAY ADVENTIST

> Behold what manner of love the Father
> has bestowed on us, that
> we should be called children of God!
> *1 John 3:1a (NKJV)*

THE FATHER
I AM A SEVENTH-DAY ADVENTIST

*But these are written that you may believe that
Jesus is the Christ, the Son of God, and that believing
you may have life in His name.*
John 20:31 (NKJV)

4

THE SON
I AM A SEVENTH-DAY ADVENTIST

> However, when He, the Spirit of truth, has come,
> He will guide you into all truth; for He will not speak
> on His own authority, but whatever He hears
> He will speak; and He will tell you things to come.
> *John 16:13 (NKJV)*

THE HOLY SPIRIT
I AM A SEVENTH-DAY ADVENTIST

> But now, O Lord, You are our Father,
> we are the clay, and You our potter;
> and all we are the work of Your hand.
> *Isaiah 64:8 (NKJV)*

THE CREATION
I AM A SEVENTH-DAY ADVENTIST

> For I know that in me (that is, in my flesh) nothing good dwells; for to will is present with me, but how to perform what is good I do not find.
> *Romans 7:18 (NKJV)*

7

NATURE OF HUMANITY
I AM A SEVENTH-DAY ADVENTIST

> In this the children of God
> and the children of the devil are manifest:
> Whoever does not practice righteousness is not of God,
> nor is he who does not love his brother.
> *1 John 3:10 (NKJV)*

> But now Christ is risen from the dead, and has become the firstfruits of those who have fallen asleep.
> *1 Corinthians 15:20 (NKJV)*

> For the Son of Man did not come
> to destroy men's lives but to save them.
> *Luke 9:56 (NKJV)*

THE EXPERIENCE OF SALVATION
I AM A SEVENTH-DAY ADVENTIST

Therefore, laying aside all malice, all deceit, hypocrisy, envy,
and all evil speaking, as newborn babes, desire
the pure milk of the word, that you may grow thereby.
1 Peter 2: 1-2 (NKJV)

THE GROWING IN CHRIST
I AM A SEVENTH-DAY ADVENTIST

> And the Lord added to the church daily those who were being saved.
> *Acts 2:47b (NKJV)*

THE CHURCH
I AM A SEVENTH-DAY ADVENTIST

Preach the word! Be ready in season and out of season. Convince, rebuke, exhort, with all longsuffering and teaching.
2 Timothy 4:2 (NKJV)

13

THE REMNANT AND ITS MISSION
I AM A SEVENTH-DAY ADVENTIST

> And the glory which You gave Me I have given them, that they may be one just as We are one: I in them, and You in Me; that they may be made perfect in one, and that the world may know that You have sent Me, and have loved them as You have loved Me.
>
> *John 17:22-23 (NKJV)*

UNITY IN THE BODY OF CHRIST
I AM A SEVENTH-DAY ADVENTIST

> And now why are you waiting? Arise and be baptized, and wash away your sins, calling on the name of the Lord.
> *Acts 22:16 (NKJV)*

BAPTISM
I AM A SEVENTH-DAY ADVENTIST

> Likewise He also took the cup after supper, saying, "This cup is the new covenant in My blood, which is shed for you."
> Luke 22:20 (NKJV)

THE LORD'S SUPPER
I AM A SEVENTH-DAY ADVENTIST

> As each one has received a gift, minister it to one another, as good stewards of the manifold grace of God.
> *1 Peter 4:10 (NKJV)*

> Yes, and all the prophets, from Samuel and those who follow, as many as have spoken, have also foretold these days.
> *Acts 3:24 (NKJV)*

THE GIFT OF PROPHECY
I AM A SEVENTH-DAY ADVENTIST

So He said to him, "Why do you call Me good? No one is good but One, that is, God. But if you want to enter into life, keep the commandments."
Matthew 19:17 (NKJV)

THE LAW OF GOD
I AM A SEVENTH-DAY ADVENTIST

> Then God blessed the seventh day and sanctified it, because in it He rested from all His work which God had created and made.
> *Genesis 2:3 (NKJV)*

THE SABBATH
I AM A SEVENTH-DAY ADVENTIST

> Give, and it will be given to you: good measure, pressed down, shaken together, and running over will be put into your bosom. For with the same measure that you use, it will be measured back to you.
> *Luke 6:38 (NKJV)*

STEWARDSHIP
I AM A SEVENTH-DAY ADVENTIST

> Therefore, as we have opportunity,
> let us do good to all, especially to
> those who are of the household of faith.
> *Galatians 6:10 (NKJV)*

CHRISTIAN BEHAVIOR
I AM A SEVENTH-DAY ADVENTIST

> Live joyfully with the wife whom you love all the days of your vain life which He has given you under the sun, all your days of vanity.
> *Ecclesiastes 9:9a (NKJV)*

For Christ has not entered the holy places made with hands, which are copies of the true, but into Heaven itself, now to appear in the presence of God for us.
Hebrews 9:24 (NKJV)

CHRIST MINISTRY IN THE HEAVENLY SANCTUARY
I AM A SEVENTH-DAY ADVENTIST

> This same Jesus, who was taken up from you into heaven, will so come in like manner as you saw Him go into heaven...
> *Acts 1:11b (NKJV)*

THE SECOND COMING OF CHRIST
I AM A SEVENTH-DAY ADVENTIST

> Do not marvel at this; for the hour is coming in which all who are in the graves will hear His voice and come forth-those who have done good, to the resurrection of life, and those who have done evil, to the resurrection of condemnation.
> *John 5:28-29 (NKJV)*

DEATH AND RESURRECTION
I AM A SEVENTH-DAY ADVENTIST

> ...But the rest of the dead did not
> live again until the thousand years were finished.
> *Revelation 20:5a (NKJV)*

> Now I saw a new heaven and a new earth, for the first heaven and the first earth had passed away. Also there was no more sea.
> *Revelation 21:1 (NKJV)*

THE NEW EARTH
I AM A SEVENTH-DAY ADVENTIST

Study References
SDA Fundamental Beliefs

1. The Holy Scriptures – Old and New Testaments, are the written word of God, given by divine inspiration. *(Ps. 119:105; Prov. 30:5, 6; Isa. 8:20; John 17:17; 1 Thess. 2:13; 2 Tim. 3:16, 17; Heb. 4:12; 2 Peter 1:20, 21)*

2. The Trinity – There is one God: Father, Son, and Holy Spirit, a unity of three co-eternal Persons. *(Gen. 1:26; Deut. 6:4; Isa. 6:8; Matt. 28:19; John 3:16 2 Cor. 1:21, 22; 13:14; Eph. 4:4-6; 1 Peter 1:2.)*

3. The Father - God the eternal Father is the Creator, Source, Sustainer, and Sovereign of all creation. He sent His son to save us from our sins and to show us what He is like. *(Gen. 1:1; Deut. 4:35; Ps. 110:1, 4; John 3:16; 14:9; 1 Cor. 15:28; 1 Tim. 1:17; 1 John 4:8; Rev. 4:11.)*

4. The Son - God the eternal Son became incarnate in Jesus Christ. Through Him all things were created, the salvation of humanity is accomplished, and the world is judged. *(Isa. 53:4-6; Dan. 9:25-27; Luke 1:35; John 1:1-3, 14; 5:22; 10:30; 14:1-3, 9, 13; Rom. 6:23; 1 Cor. 15:3, 4; 2 Cor. 3:18; 5:17-19; Phil. 2:5-11; Col. 1:15-19; Heb. 2:9-18; 8:1, 2.)*

5. The Holy Spirit – God the eternal Spirit was active with the Father and the Son in Creation, incarnation, and redemption. He inspired the writers of Scripture. The Holy Spirit empowers us and guides our understanding. The Spirit touches our hearts and transforms us, renewing the image of God in which we were created. *(Gen. 1:1, 2; 2 Sam. 23:2; Ps. 51:11; Isa. 61:1; Luke 1:35; 4:18; John 14:16-18, 26; 15:26; 16:7-13; Acts 1:8; 5:3; 10:38; Rom. 5:5; 1 Cor. 12:7-11; 2 Cor. 3:18; 2 Peter 1:21.)*

6. Creation – God created the universe. In a six-day creation the Lord made "the heavens and the earth, the sea, and all that is in them" and rested on the seventh day. Thus, He established the Sabbath as a perpetual memorial of the work He performed. *(Gen. 1-2; 5; 11; Exod. 20:8-11; Ps. 19:1-6; 33:6, 9; 104; Isa. 45:12, 18; Acts 17:24; Col. 1:16; Heb. 1:2; 11:3; Rev. 10:6; 14:7.)*

7. Nature of Humanity – Man and woman were made in the image of God with individuality, the power and freedom to think and to do. Once molded in God's image, now fractured by sin, it took a perfect Savior to reconcile us. The Spirit restores God's reflection within us so God can work through us. *(Gen. 1:26-28; 2:7, 15; 3; Ps. 8:4-8; 51:5, 10; 58:3; Jer. 17:9; Acts 17:24-28; Rom. 5:12-17; 2 Cor. 5:19, 20; Eph. 2:3; 1 Thess. 5:23; 1 John 3:4; 4:7, 8, 11, 20.)*

8. The Great Controversy – All humanity is now involved in a great controversy between Christ and Satan regarding the character of God, His law, and His sovereignty over the universe. This conflict originated in heaven when a created being, endowed with freedom of choice, in self-exaltation became Satan, God's adversary, and led into rebellion a portion of the angels. He introduced the spirit of rebellion into this world when he led Adam and Eve into sin. *(Gen. 3; 6-8; Job 1:6-12; Isa. 14:12-14; Ezek. 28:12-18; Rom. 1:19-32; 3:4; 5:12-21; 8:19-22; 1 Cor. 4:9; Heb. 1:14; 1 Peter 5:8; 2 Peter 3:6; Rev. 12:4-9.)*

9. The Life, Death, and Resurrection of Christ – In Christ's life of perfect obedience to God's will, His suffering, death, and resurrection, God provided the only means of atonement for human sin, so that those who by faith accept this atonement may have eternal life. *(Gen. 3:15; Ps. 22:1; Isa. 53; John 3:16; 14:30; Rom. 1:4; 3:25; 4:25; 8:3, 4; 1 Cor. 15:3, 4, 20-22; 2 Cor. 5:14, 15, 19-21; Phil. 2:6-11; Col. 2:15; 1 Peter 2:21, 22; 1 John 2:2; 4:10.)*

10. The Experience of Salvation – In infinite love and mercy God made Christ, who knew no sin, to be sin for us, so that in Him we might be made the righteousness of God. When we accept God's grace and salvation, the Holy Spirit reveals our need for Jesus and re-creates us. The Spirit builds our faith and helps us leave our broken lives behind. *(Gen. 3:15; Isa. 45:22; 53; Jer. 31:31-34; Ezek. 33:11; 36:25-27; Hab. 2:4; Mark 9:23, 24; John 3:3-8, 16; 16:8; Rom. 3:21-26; 8:1-4, 14-17; 5:6-10; 10:17; 12:2; 2 Cor. 5:17-21; Gal. 1:4; 3:13, 14, 26; 4:4-7; Eph. 2:4-10; Col. 1:13, 14; Titus 3:3-7; Heb. 8:7-12; 1 Peter 1:23; 2:21, 22; 2 Peter 1:3, 4; Rev. 13:8.)*

11. The Growing in Christ – By His death on the cross Jesus triumphed over the forces of evil. Jesus' victory gives us victory over the evil forces that still seek to control us. In this new freedom in Jesus, we are called to grow into the likeness of His character. We are also called to follow Christ's example by compassionately ministering to the physical, mental, social, emotional, and spiritual needs of humanity. *(1 Chron. 29:11; Ps. 1:1, 2; 23:4; 77:11, 12; Matt. 20:25-28; 25:31-46; Luke 10:17-20; John 20:21; Rom. 8:38, 39; 2 Cor. 3:17, 18; Gal. 5:22-25; Eph. 5:19, 20; 6:12-18; Phil. 3:7-14; Col. 1:13, 14; 2:6, 14, 15; 1 Thess. 5:16-18, 23; Heb. 10:25; James 1:27; 2 Peter 2:9; 3:18; 1 John 4:4.)*

12. The Church – The church is the community of believers who confess Jesus Christ as Lord and Saviour. Looking to Jesus as its leader and Redeemer, the church is called to take the good news of salvation to all. *(Gen. 12:1-3; Exod. 19:3-7; Matt. 16:13-20; 18:18; 28:19, 20; Acts 2:38-42; 7:38; 1 Cor. 1:2; Eph. 1:22, 23; 2:19-22; 3:8-11; 5:23-27; Col. 1:17, 18; 1 Peter 2:9.)*

13. The Remnant and Its Mission – At the end of time, God will call His people back to core truths. This remnant announces the arrival of the judgment hour, proclaims salvation through Christ, and heralds the approach of His second advent. *(Dan. 7:9-14; Isa. 1:9; 11:11; Jer. 23:3; Mic. 2:12; 2 Cor. 5:10; 1 Peter 1:16-19; 4:17; 2 Peter 3:10-14; Jude 3, 14; Rev. 12:17; 14:6-12; 18:1-4.)*

14. Unity in the Body of Christ – The church is one body with many members, called from every nation, kindred, tongue, and people. We are all equal in Christ, who by one Spirit has bonded us into one fellowship with Him and with one another; we are to serve and be served without partiality or reservation. *(Ps. 133:1; Matt. 28:19, 20; John 17:20-23; Acts 17:26, 27; Rom. 12:4, 5; 1 Cor. 12:12-14; 2 Cor. 5:16, 17; Gal. 3:27 29; Eph. 2:13-16; 4:3-6, 11-16; Col. 3:10-15.)*

15. Baptism – Baptism is a symbol of our union with Christ, the forgiveness of our sins, and our reception of the Holy Spirit. *(Matt. 28:19, 20; Acts 2:38; 16:30-33; 22:16; Rom. 6:1-6; Gal. 3:27; Col. 2:12, 13.)*

16. The Lord's Supper – The Lord's Supper is a participation in the emblems of the body and blood of Jesus as an expression of faith in Him, our Lord and Saviour. *(Matt. 26:17-30; John 6:48-63; 13:1-17; 1 Cor. 10:16, 17; 11:23-30; Rev. 3:20.)*

17. Spiritual Gifts and Ministries – God bestows upon all members of His church in every age spiritual gifts that each member is to use in loving ministry for the common good of the church and of humanity. Given by the agency of the Holy Spirit, who apportions to each member as He wills, the gifts provide all abilities and ministries needed by the church to fulfill its divinely ordained functions. *(Acts 6:1-7; Rom. 12:4-8; 1 Cor. 12:7-11, 27, 28; Eph. 4:8, 11-16; 1 Tim. 3:1-13; 1 Peter 4:10, 11.)*

18. The Gift of Prophecy – The Scriptures testify that one of the gifts of the Holy Spirit is prophecy. In the last days, as in biblical times, the Holy Spirit has blessed God's people with the gift of prophecy. One who demonstrated this gift was Ellen G. White, a founder of the Seventh-day Adventist church. *(Num. 12:6; 2 Chron. 20:20; Amos 3:7; Joel 2:28, 29; Acts 2:14-21; 2 Tim. 3:16, 17; Heb. 1:1-3; Rev. 12:17; 19:10; 22:8, 9.)*

19. The Law of God – The great principles of God's law are embodied in the Ten Commandments and exemplified in the life of Christ. They express God's love, will, and purposes concerning human conduct and relationships and are binding upon all people in every age. These precepts are the basis of God's covenant with His people and the standard in God's judgment. *(Exod. 20:1-17; Deut. 28:1-14; Ps. 19:7-14; 40:7, 8; Matt. 5:17-20; 22:36-40; John 14:15; 15:7-10; Rom. 8:3, 4; Eph. 2:8-10; Heb. 8:8-10; 1 John 2:3; 5:3; Rev. 12:17; 14:12.)*

20. The Sabbath – The gracious Creator, after the six days of Creation, rested on the seventh day and instituted the Sabbath for all people as a memorial of Creation. The seventh day was set aside as the day of rest, worship, and ministry in harmony with the teaching and practice of Jesus, the Lord of the Sabbath. *(Gen. 2:1-3; Exod. 20:8-11; 31:13-17; Lev. 23:32; Deut. 5:12-15; Isa. 56:5, 6; 58:13, 14; Ezek. 20:12, 20; Matt. 12:1-12; Mark 1:32; Luke 4:16; Heb. 4:1-11.)*

21. Stewardship – We are God's stewards, entrusted by Him with time and opportunities, abilities and possessions, and the blessings of the earth and its resources. We are responsible to Him for their proper use. (Gen. 1:26-28; 2:15; 1 Chron. 29:14; Haggai 1:3-11; Mal. 3:8-12; Matt. 23:23; Rom. 15:26, 27; 1 Cor. 9:9-14; 2 Cor. 8:1-15; 9:7.)

22. Christian Behavior – We are called to be a godly people who think, feel, and act in harmony with biblical principles in all aspects of personal and social life. Through the Holy Spirit we glorify God in our minds, bodies and spirits. (Gen. 7:2; Exod. 20:15; Lev. 11:1-47; Ps. 106:3; Rom. 12:1, 2; 1 Cor. 6:19, 20; 10:31; 2 Cor. 6:14-7:1; 10:5; Eph. 5:1-21; Phil. 2:4; 4:8; 1 Tim. 2:9, 10; Titus 2:11, 12; 1 Peter 3:1-4; 1 John 2:6; 3 John 2.)

23. Marriage and the Family – Marriage was divinely established in Eden and affirmed by Jesus to be a lifelong union between a man and a woman in loving companionship. (Gen. 2:18-25; Exod. 20:12; Deut. 6:5-9; Prov. 22:6; Mal. 4:5, 6; Matt. 5:31, 32; 19:3-9, 12; Mark 10:11, 12; John 2:1-11; 1 Cor. 7:7, 10, 11; 2 Cor. 6:14; Eph. 5:21-33; 6:1-4.)

24. Christ's Ministry in the Heavenly Sanctuary – There is a sanctuary in heaven, the true tabernacle that the Lord set up and not humans. In it Christ ministers on our behalf, making available to believers the benefits of His atoning sacrifice offered once and for all on the cross. (Lev. 16; Num. 14:34; Ezek. 4:6; Dan. 7:9-27; 8:13, 14; 9:24-27; Heb. 1:3; 2:16, 17; 4:14-16; 8:1-5; 9:11-28; 10:19-22; Rev. 8:3-5; 11:19; 14:6, 7; 20:12; 14:12; 22:11, 12.)

25. The Second Coming of Christ – The second coming of Christ is the blessed hope of the church, the grand climax of the gospel. The Saviour's coming will be literal, personal, visible, and worldwide. (Matt. 24; Mark 13; Luke 21; John 14:1-3; Acts 1:9-11; 1 Cor. 15:51-54; 1 Thess. 4:13-18; 5:1-6; 2 Thess. 1:7-10; 2:8; 2 Tim. 3:1-5; Titus 2:13; Heb. 9:28; Rev. 1:7; 14:14-20; 19:11-21.)

26. Death and Resurrection – The wages of sin is death. But God, who alone is immortal, will grant eternal life to His redeemed. Until that day death is an unconscious state for all people. The unconscious nothingness of death separates us from the God of life, yet Jesus' defeat of death means the saved can look forward to resurrection and living forever. (Job 19:25-27; Ps. 146:3, 4; Eccl. 9:5, 6, 10; Dan. 12:2, 13; Isa. 25:8; John 5:28, 29; 11:11-14; Rom. 6:23; 6:16; 1 Cor. 15:51-54; Col. 3:4; 1 Thess. 4:13-17; 1 Tim. 6:15; Rev. 20:1-10.) declare that God is love; and He shall reign forever. (Isa. 35; 65:17-25; Matt. 5:5; 2 Peter 3:13; Rev. 11:15; 21:1-7; 22:1-5.)

27. The Millennium and the End of Sin – The millennium is the thousand-year reign of Christ with His saints in heaven between the first and second resurrections. During this time the wicked dead will be judged; the earth will be utterly desolate, without living human inhabitants, but occupied by Satan and his angels. *(Rev. 20; 1 Cor. 6:2, 3; Jer. 4:23-26; Rev. 21:1-5; Mal. 4:1; Eze. 28:18, 19.)*

28. The New Earth – God will recreate a new heaven and a new earth. Jesus lives with us forever. On the new earth, in which righteousness dwells, God will provide an eternal home for the redeemed. The great controversy will be ended, and sin will be no more. All things, animate and inanimate, will declare that God is love; and He shall reign forever. *(Isa. 35; 65:17-25; Matt. 5:5; 2 Peter 3:13; Rev. 11:15; 21:1-7; 22:1-5.)*

Source: https://www.adventist.org/en/beliefs/

www.ingramcontent.com/pod-product-compliance
Lightning Source LLC
Chambersburg PA
CBHW060046230426
43661CB00004B/682